Who You Were Meant to Be

Zoe McKey is a Communication and Lifestyle Coach based in Los Angeles, California.

She studied in international and social studies for her bachelor's and master's degrees. Being an avid student of human behaviour, psychology, and healthy connections, she has spent more than 400 hours in therapy, journaled 1000+ pages, and read over 300 books on the topics of communication, self-discovery, and self-improvement.

For 10 years, she's been helping people discover how to live the life they want. Zoe has a profound understanding on what it takes to gain self-understanding, get unstuck, and reach new levels of growth and fulfilment. She has written over 30 books on these subjects that have been translated in multiple languages around the globe.

Who You Were Meant to Be

Become the Best Version of Yourself

ZOE MCKEY

Published by
Rupa Publications India Pvt. Ltd 2024
7/16, Ansari Road, Daryaganj
New Delhi 110002

Sales centres:
Bengaluru Chennai
Hyderabad Jaipur Kathmandu
Kolkata Mumbai Prayagraj

Copyright © Zoe McKey 2024
Published under arrangement with Zoe McKey through TLL Literary Agency

The views and opinions expressed in this book are the author's
own and the facts are as reported by her which have been
verified to the extent possible, and the publishers are not in
any way liable for the same.

All rights reserved.
No part of this publication may be reproduced, transmitted,
or stored in a retrieval system, in any form or by any means,
electronic, mechanical, photocopying, recording or otherwise,
without the prior permission of the publisher.

P-ISBN: 978-93-5702-856-1
E-ISBN: 978-93-5702-914-8

First impression 2024

10 9 8 7 6 5 4 3 2 1

The moral right of the author has been asserted.

Printed in India

This book is sold subject to the condition that it shall not, by way of
trade or otherwise, be lent, resold, hired out, or otherwise circulated,
without the publisher's prior consent, in any form of binding or
cover other than that in which it is published.

Contents

1. What Brought You to This Book? — 1
2. On Personality — 20
3. Freud vs. Jung — 30
4. Gary Chapman's Languages — 45
5. Temperament Types — 62
6. Find Something that Defines You — 76

Closing Words — 90
References — 92
Endnotes — 95

1
What Brought You to This Book?

In the age of social media where the 'perfect life' flashes on our phone screens daily, it is almost inevitable to feel inferior and inadequate. We develop thoughts of self-doubt, powerlessness, and shame. We feel frustrated because we think that our lives are mediocre compared to others. From there, our thoughts go spiraling downwards and before we know it, we have already created the feeling of not being enough.

While a lot of people experience this just once in a while, for some, such negative feelings could pop up with regular occurrence. Self-loathing can get so bad that it vanishes our self-esteem, weakens our relationships, and hinders our productivity. Feelings of self-doubt, shame, and inadequacy can also strip our true identity away leaving us with a superficial notion of being so much less than others.

If you are someone who can relate to the paragraphs above, you have come to the right place. In this book, we are going to talk about discovering your real self, how to cope with feelings of inadequacy, how to improve your relationship with others and yourself, your temperament, character-specific desires when it comes to love, and much more. This book does not guarantee that your worries will magically go away, but rather, it aims to serve as a companion and advisor as you go through them.

Feeling of Inadequacy

In our everyday life, we can inevitably find ourselves in situations where our self-esteem feels attacked. Whether it be intentional or not, triggers can be encountered even in places we consider safe. Take for example your home. One negative comment from your mom about your weight can easily trigger shame and jeopardize your confidence. Even a bit of a reprimand from your spouse regarding your neatness can instantly make you doubt yourself, the security of your relationship.

While these triggering situations can really stimulate feelings of inadequacy, most of the time this insidious self-perception can already be present in our system for a long time. An individual's low self-image can stem from unpleasant childhood experiences, family problems, abusive relationships and similar emotionally damaging events. Furthermore, social media is also one of the biggest prompts of self-doubt. The message it portrays and the unrealistic standards it sets can cause overwhelming thoughts of anxiety and lacking.

Feeling of inadequacy often translates to:

- Trust issues.
- Anxiety.

What Brought You to This Book?

- Reluctance to show or accept affection.
- Paranoia.
- Inability to accept compliments or criticisms.
- Fear of rejection and failure.
- Conflict avoidance.[1]

When you start questioning your self-worth, you start to question everything else about you and your actions. You judge yourself multiple times a day without noticing it; even when you are just doing the most mundane tasks as dishwashing. Irrational thoughts of being not good enough are constantly present in your mind.

You cannot help but compare yourself to others. Most of the time, we are too engrossed in what social media shows us that we forget that these pictures do not equate to real life. When you see your 'successful' friends post on Facebook or Instagram, you think that their lives are way better than yours and that you are left far behind.

What we fail to see is that everybody can be just as insecure as we are. Usually, the people who show off the most are the ones who are in most need of validation. We all have our own ways—negative or not—of proving ourselves. At present, social media is the biggest outlet that we use for self-promotion— which often stems from the deepest fear of inadequacy and the most desperate need to be seen and acknowledged. Many of the chain-posters have the belief that if people see their photos and get jealous of their seemingly-perfect life they achieved some kind of acknowledgement from their peers. They fail to notice that the very foundation they seek attention for is unreal, superficial, and likes will never fill up their empty emotional tank craving for human connection.

There are other kind of attention seekers on social media—those who overshare. They wish to establish connection with people by leashing out in a post about the injustice they experienced, the pain their cheating partner put them through, or they just say, 'Hey, I feel very sad now. Can someone PM (private message) me?' If you can identify with any of these actions, know that you're not the only one doing this. And rest assured, I'm not here to shame you. I feel your pain. You are probably struggling to make friends, really wish to connect but something prevents you to do it in real life (hint, sense of inadequacy) so you try what you can online. If you get rejected, it's a less tangible experience than being shamed or humiliated face to face. You wish to put yourself out there and 'save yourself from out there' at the same time. I hope this book will provide you some information on how to be out there, ready to good and bad feedback and not put your self-worth dependant on either of them.

It is very important to remind ourselves that fulfillment and happiness mean different things for everybody. We all have our own storylines we are comfortable to share and our shames we try to hide at all cost. Ultimately, we all have our own struggles that we naturally do not want to show.

When we feel less of who we really are, we tend to seek for validation in all the wrong places. We fall into toxic, self-sabotaging cycles like binge eating, overspending, overworking, and snapping at the smallest things. In other cases we turn to other numbing sources like alcohol, drugs, and medication. Some people start becoming distant to their friends and family. Others dangerously enter a relationship thinking that their partner will fill their void.

Our worth can never be handed to us or mended by another person. Our worth has always been within us and will always be for us to find. Realizing our real value is an intrinsic process which involves a lot of self-monitoring, and contemplation. It is not a social activity—at least not the very beginning—but rather a practice that we do alone, with ourselves.

How to Cope with Feelings of Inadequacy

A person who has serious issues of low self-esteem always manages to antagonize himself. He does not give himself recognition for his achievements. He downplays his strengths. He does not consider himself successful or even worthy of anything. Lastly, he feels guilty when he feels happy about something because he thinks the happiness is undeserved. Or he may feel a deep anxiety whenever he allows himself to be content as a dark voice starts whispering, 'you know tragedy is coming. It's coming. It will strike you and your stupid happiness soon.' Then he becomes terrified of the coming tragedy, numbs his happiness to be 'prepared' to the sorrow that will come. He doesn't realize that sorrow just storke in, just by this very self-sabotaging thought.

When coping with feelings of inadequacy, the first thing to do is to build tolerance for positive feelings. You have to train yourself to welcome positive feelings. Instead of dodging compliments or affection, try to teach yourself this key phrase: *'I deserve this.'* When you start feeling pride, joy or any other positive feeling, your mind can trick you into believing that you are not worthy of it. Shift your focus to the *I-deserve-this* attitude.

There are many tangible ways to cope with negative feelings and thoughts. From different mantras to exercises, you have a wide array of choices to train your mind. Take power posing as an example. Social psychologist Amy Cuddy published a research on how doing the 'power pose' creates a sense of empowerment on our body and mind.

In case you are wondering, power pose is an expansive gesture of putting your hands on your waist (imagine the Wonder Woman pose). She said that our body language governs our own thoughts and feelings. Thus, sporting such powerful stance can signal a boost in self-esteem. On the part of hard science, her research showed that those who regularly did the power pose experienced an increase in testosterone and decrease in cortisol. These hormonal changes can be attributed to feelings of power.[2]

Simple exercises like a morning run also help a lot in getting your adrenaline flowing. Exercising does not only energize the body but also the mind. Breathing exercises or yoga is a good way of training your mind too. You just find the approach that best suits you and be open to lifestyle changes.

The Change Triangle

The Change Triangle is a map that will carry you from a place of disconnection back to your true self (Hendel, 2018). The term was first coined by David Malan as 'Triangle of Conflict' which later on developed to 'Triangle of Experience' by Diana Fosha. Basically, this triangle represents our core emotions, inhibitory emotions and defenses.[3]

Our core emotions are our reactive emotions. This means that these are the feelings we naturally get from a certain environment. Driven by a stimulus, the core emotions are feelings of fear, joy, and anger, among others.

Inhibitory emotions are feelings that block our core emotions. If there is conflict or an overwhelming core emotion, we tend to resist feeling them. Two main examples of inhibitory emotions are shame and guilt.

Lastly, defenses are a much higher level of resistance. They block both core and inhibitory emotions. Depression can be one example where we simply reject to acknowledge any type of emotion. Other defense can include sarcasm, joking, spacing out, and anything that can disregard our emotions.

Visualizing the Change Triangle, two of its components—inhibitory emotions and defenses—each sit at both sides of the triangle. At the base is its third component, the core emotions.

Now that we know what consists the Change Triangle, you might ask: how does it actually work?

When you are faced with any stressful situation, the first thing to do is to identify where you are on the triangle. Are you feeling the core emotions, an inhibitory emotion, or are your defenses already up? After figuring out where you are, you need to decide where you need to go on the triangle. Imagine a triangle where the right and left sides are the defenses and inhibitory emotions, while the base is the core emotions.

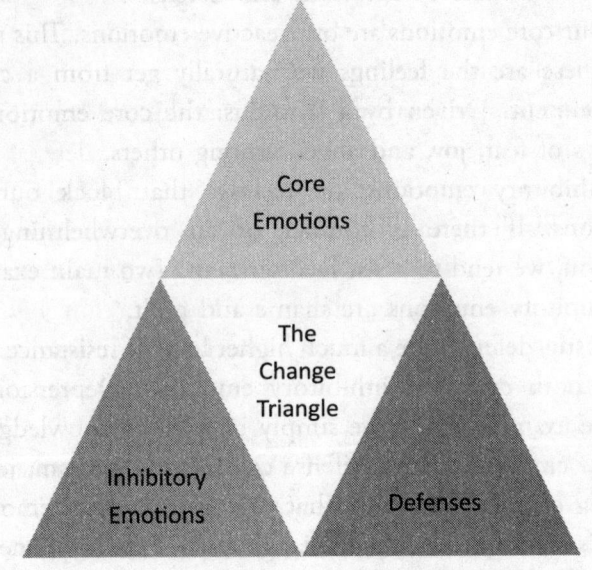

Picture I: The Change Triangle

Your goal is to get to the top whether clockwise or counter-clockwise. After getting in touch with your core emotions, you will feel the authenticity of your emotions as these emotions allow you to be in your natural state. After getting to the core emotions, your last step is to get to the state where your heart is open for your authentic self. This means that you have already reached calmness, confidence, and clarity.

How the Change Triangle Works in Real Life

Imagine a person who is going to her first ever job interview. Of course, she would be nervous. Anxiety can ensue which is an inhibitory emotion. But the moment thoughts like 'I can't do this' or 'Maybe I should just skip this' come across her mind, it means that she is already on the defenses side. She is trying to get away from everything she feels.

Moving from the inhibitory side to the defenses side of the triangle, she needs to find her way to the base: the core emotions. Finding your natural state of emotion will make you get more in touch with your core feeling. In our example, the core emotion is fear—which leads to nervousness then to anxiety.

The acknowledgement of your fear is one crucial step in assessing the situation. Now that you find the real reason of your anxiety, the next thing to do is to analyze the core emotion (fear). *What will happen to me if this fear comes true? Is it the end? Is it the worst-case scenario?* More often than not, the answer to these questions is not something crazy bad. You will then realize that your fear is just caused by overthinking.

From there, you can employ different approaches to confront fear. As mentioned, you can go from reciting mantras, to power posing or physical exercises. The important part is that you learn to live in harmony with your core emotions. After that, it will be easier to manage any challenging situation.

Three Practices

Developing feelings of inadequacy can either be on an impulse or can be deeply rooted in a person's childhood. When I say on an impulse, it means that the feeling of self-doubt can naturally come in momentary situations like being nervous for a contest or being in a room full of people that you deem to be richer, smarter or more prominent than you. These conditions are fleeting; thus, the feeling of inadequacy can come and go.

It is a different case if the feeling of inadequacy is formed through childhood. Individuals who generally have low self-esteem regardless of the situation they are in at the moment usually had issues growing up. For example, a child born into a family of doctors is most probably expected to be a doctor. This expectation does not only come from the family but also from the society's stereotypes. If the child develops interest in arts instead of medicine, he might feel that he is lacking something compared to his parents. He will wonder why he is different from his family. He might think that he has no skills or he is not trying hard enough to become a doctor. He sees himself as weak when in fact he just became interested in other things which is perfectly normal.

The environment we grow up in holds a great impact on our self-image. High-pressure environments usually produce individuals with general feelings of inadequacy. It is because they grew up struggling to keep up with the high standards set by the people around them. The nature of the society, as well as religion, also play a big part in how people develop their self-esteem.

The Compensation Trap[4]

Austrian psychologist Alfred Adler firmly believed that the feeling of inadequacy is the major motivator of human behavior and psychology. We are prompted to strive even harder during the times we feel inadequate. When we develop an inferiority complex, we tend to also develop a strong desire to be better than everyone else.

Adler called this behavior as 'overcompensation.' We can feel that it is not enough being equal with everyone. We want to be number one. We are blinded by the thought that the only way to get rid of the feeling of inadequacy is when we become better than the people who we now consider better than us. We desperately want to turn off our inferiority complex that is why we choose to overcompensate.

It is called overcompensation instead of compensation for this reason—we need to outdo others, not just be equal with them.

You might have heard of stories where the once bullied boy later on becomes the bully. Why does this happen? One would think that bullied people should rather avoid bullying as it was so painful for them to endure, too. The counterintuitive 'bullied becomes the bully' phenomenon happens because being inferior creates a very unpleasant feeling. This triggers the individual to fight to overcome it. When a person is bullied, his perceived overcoming can manifest in forms of machismo. He can even change his physique, how he speaks and how he carries himself overall. He does not want to be stepped on anymore, so he aims to be the number one bully so nobody can touch him.

This overcompensation can be a trap because it is a betrayal of one's true self. We leave our old selves to find a new self that will fit the unreasonable or unhealthy standards we set for ourselves out of fear. This can lead us to living an unnatural life.

No Such Thing as Normal

When we say there is no such thing as normal, it means that there is no standard way of living. Everybody lives their own comfort and challenges. There is no formula that can be used to get a perfect life because a perfect life is non-existent. Our lives are not absolute. The world is not just black and white.

Whenever you feel inadequate, try asking yourself: inadequate compared to whom? If a person with a seemingly good life comes into your mind, ask yourself: is he really living a perfect life? Is his way of living the ultimate way of living? For sure, your answer will be no. Because there will be people who can be considered 'better' than him.

This is life. We think that the people around us are living the perfect life, but underneath the neat surface are those imperfections we do not see. Even the people in history we consider as great role models had their fair share of mistakes and struggles: Winston Churchill was an alcoholic, Thomas Jefferson had around 600 slaves during his lifetime,[5] and Mahatma Gandhi—someone who widely preached chastity—had an affair for years.

All You Can Be Is You

As cliché as it may sound, the key to living a fulfilling life is to just be yourself. Comparing yourself to others is nothing but a detrimental behavior. You have to accept that every person lives with his or her own strengths and weaknesses. You have to be accepting of your limitations and nurturing of your skills. Remember that it is okay if someone is better than you at something. In another case, you can also be considered better than someone else. It just goes round and round.

The important thing is that you live up to your own standards. Identify the things that you think are important in living a good life. Are you working towards them? Good. Do not seek approval from people who do not even know what your goals are. Only you know what you need. The only person you need to beat is your previous self. Strive to be better than the you of yesterday.

The Paradox of Self-Discovery

When we ask the question 'who am I?' it is usually closely followed by another one namely, 'what's my purpose?' This question is just as hard to answer as the former, so we start jumping back and forth between these questions, trying to explain one with the other.

We hope if we find out who we are, it will actually give us a purpose. Or if we find our purpose, that will illuminate who we are. We get so preoccupied answering these questions that we won't even realize life is passing us by. We'll end up waking with the torment of these questions at the age of fifty, feeling depressed that we still don't know our higher purpose, that magnificent aim with which we came to this Earth. It's so inconceivable that after such a long search, such a fierce road of self-discovery, so many personality tests and books, we still don't know how to answer these questions.

What if insisting on answering these questions just pushes us away from the real questions and answers we should focus on?

We have a limited time to live on this Earth. Some more than others, but game over will hit all of us at some point. Between start and game over, we do things. Some of these things are important, but most of them are not. Even among the important things we do, just a few people get to do their 'purpose' on a worldwide level.

Whoever we are—or whoever we become—is mostly defined by the most important events we experience during our lifetime. These events make us happy, give us meaning, and ultimately form who we are. Instead of focusing on finding a purpose or knowing who you are—in order to find a purpose—ry to answer this question:

What are the most important things for me to spend my time on?[6]

This is a much easier question to answer, and with a little contemplation, you can arrive to an answer. Weirdly enough, by the time you answer it, you'll get a somewhat clearer picture of the person you are and what activities are good enough to consider making them your purpose.

We tend to over-mystify the entire self-discovery process, mostly because of our own self-importance. 'This is a life and death question; the answer can't be simple!' Yes, it can, and actually, it is. I know, it sounds insulting in today's culture, where everything from face cream commercials to Oprah enhances individual uniqueness. But the sooner you accept that you and I, and any other person really, are not that special after all, the sooner you'll deconstruct that wall of complexity that robs you from the genuine purpose of human life—happiness. When you start searching for meaning or purpose in the simplest things, you'll be shocked how much you will find.

To procure a breakthrough in self-knowledge, you need to change your current way of approaching the question 'who am I?' For one reason or another, your searching for answers didn't bear fruit until now. Otherwise you'd know who you are and you wouldn't read this book.

If you feel something's off with your approach so far, you're probably right. No matter how well you are doing, how healthy you are, how much love you are surrounded with, as long as you're tormented by the questions 'who am I?' and 'what's my purpose?' you won't be able to appreciate them. Even if at the end of the road, you'll realize that these everyday things are the true meaning of life and you had them all along.

You can try to change the self-discovery path you're walking on by contemplating on answers to the question, *'What are the most important things for me to spend my time on?'*

The Road Back to You

Getting in touch with the most important things in your life to spend time on is not an easy feat. You have to really dig deep and identify numerous things about yourself—your needs, wants, defense mechanisms, insecurities, and talents. You also have to identify your thought process and to what degree is it influenced by the outside world.

What Brought You to This Book?

Do you like the things you like because you really find them good or just because your best friend also likes it?

Do you agree with the political and religious views of your parents?

Do you just say something because your professor said so?

Sometimes the world can be so noisy that our voice gets drowned. When life feels too overwhelming, find solitude. Today it is suggested that being alone is uncool and that loners are losers, but you have to remind yourself that it is not true. It is okay to dine alone. It is okay to watch a movie alone. Giving yourself your own time is the best gift. These are the moments where you can contemplate about a your life and what you truly want to do with it without being influenced by others.

As we talk about contemplation, one way of really getting a deeper understanding of yourself is by asking good questions. Ask yourself deep questions about life and observe how your mind forms your answers. This will tell you a lot about your principles and values. Think of this activity as a mental exercise.

What types of questions should you ask yourself? Try to focus on aspects that are close to you. Whether it be financial stability, or creating meaningful relationships, you have to constantly ask 'what if' and then eventually turn these what if's to 'what is'—making your aspirations a thing of the present, your reality.

Some of these sample questions are:

'What if I pursued my childhood dream instead of settling for this job? Would I be happier?'

'What if I lose everything I have now, who is the first person I turn to?'

'What if I'm given an opportunity to live in another country, will I take it? Am I ready?'

These questions will surely make you reconsider your priorities and how you approach different life dilemmas. It is a good exercise for you to always be in touch with your internal desires and even internal conflicts.

Lastly, let go of the need to be liked by everyone. As the saying goes, you can be the most delicious peach in the world, but there's always somebody who doesn't like peaches. Maintaining relationships with other people means having misunderstandings, disappointment, and even envy. People have the tendency to feel threatened when someone is doing better than them. If you feel like the people around you do not support you when you change for the better, then it might be time to surround yourself with people who are more compatible with the new you. Remember that when it comes to being your true self: those who mind don't matter, and those who matter don't mind.

Now you are one step closer to discovering your true self. This book will take you on a journey of finding your true personality, strengths, weaknesses, and temperament. Not merely relying on metaphors, this book presents different psychology theories that are strongly founded by scientist to help you understand better how your mind works.

2
On Personality

What Is Personality?

The word 'personality' gets thrown around us daily more often than we notice. We hear, '*You have a great personality!*' or even defend ourselves with, '*Meh, this is just my personality.*' While we know what personality means on the surface, taking a much closer look at this concept will make us understand human psychology better.

Etymology-wise, the word personality came from the Latin word *persona* which refers to a theatrical mask worn by performers to either project different roles or disguise their identities. Psychologists simply define personality as the pattern of thoughts, feelings and behaviors which make an individual unique. These patterns are deemed consistent throughout a person's life.

To help you understand better, here are other definitions from different psychologists:[1]

Walter Mischel (1999)—'*(Personality is) the distinctive patterns of behavior (including thoughts and well as 'affects,'* *that is, feelings, and emotions and actions) that characterize each individual enduringly'.*

Funder (2001)—*'Personality refers to individuals' characteristic patterns of thought, emotion, and behavior, together with the psychological mechanisms—hidden or not—behind those patterns.'*

Feist and Feist (2009)—*'Personality is a pattern of relatively permanent traits and unique characteristics that give both consistency and individuality to a person's behavior.'*

American Psychology Association—*'The study of personality focuses on two broad areas: One is understanding individual differences in particular personality characteristics, such as sociability or irritability. The other is understanding how the various parts of a person come together as a whole.'*

In these varying approaches, you can see that the underlying concept behind personality remains to be the thinking patterns of an individual. These patterns can be genetically explained as well as environmentally. From genes to culture, there are a lot of influences that can form and change one's personality traits.

Components of Personality

You might be wondering, what exactly comprises a person's personality? Aside from mental and emotional patterns, fundamental characteristics of a personality include:

Consistency—For a trait to be considered a part of the personality, it should occur frequently under similar situations. This means that a person reacts the same way (with little to no variations) when presented a certain circumstance.

Psychological and physiological—While a personality is heavily influenced by psychological processes, plenty of researches suggest that it is also formed through physical (biological) processes and needs.

Impact on behaviors and actions—Personality is not just intrinsic, it affects how we behave and prompts us to do certain actions.

Multiple expressions—Personality also manifests itself in the types of relationships we make, how we present ourselves to public, and other social interactions.[2]

Furthermore, personality is also defined through statistically-identified factors called **The Big Five**.[3] These factors are much heavier on the genetics side and are generally stable over time. Let's take a closer look at The Big Five:

1. **Openness to Experience** (Inventive–Curious vs. Consistent–Cautious)
   We all know that there are people who love adventures and take risks. There are also those who play it safe and stay in their comfort zone. This pertains to an individual's openness to various life experiences. Someone who is inventive and curious is likely to

have a more active cognitive processes and can explore different ways to solve a specific problem. A person who is consistent/cautious is more comfortable going by the books and following rules.

2. **Conscientiousness**—(Efficient–Organized vs. Easy-going–Carefree)

   Conscientiousness shows the degree of spontaneity of a certain individual. Efficient and organized people like to have control over things. They are the people who plan things from day one. They feel the need to follow a certain structure and can have some perfectionist tendencies. Easy-going and carefree people on the other hand, do not dwell on the process as much—as long as the job gets done. They see things at a bird's eye view rather than zooming in on the nitty-gritty details.

3. **Extraversion**—(Outgoing–Energetic vs. Solitary–Reserved)

   Surely, you have heard of the extrovert–introvert dichotomy. Extraversion is an individual's capacity to engage in social interactions. It refers to sociability, energy and friendliness. Extroverts are more outgoing and can be impulsive when it comes to making decisions. This means that they sometimes take risks without really weighing the consequences. Conversely, introverts like to work individually or with a few select people. They do not like being the center of attention and look at things with an inward perspective.

4. **Agreeableness**—(Friendly–Compassionate vs. Cold–Unkind)
   Being an agreeable person means you show open-mindedness and compassion towards people. You are easy to talk to and cooperate well. People often perceive you as someone who is amicable and easy to work with. A person who is cold can be deemed to be unkind and selfish. This person may lack empathy and does not really care about his surroundings. This trait can undeniably cause problems with forming relationships with other people.
5. **Neuroticism**—(Sensitive–Nervous vs. Secure–Confident)
   In general, neuroticism refers to a person's emotional stability and capacity to handle different situations (e.g. stress). Sensitive, highly emotional people are much more vulnerable to pressure. In most cases, these are the people who have underlying issues with confidence and self-esteem. Those who are secure do not get easily affected with their environment. They have a strong foundation of emotional senses and can decide well even under high pressure.

Theories

Now let's talk about theories on how a personality develops. Note that these theories are an amalgamation of different schools of thought in psychology. Studies of different psychologists were gathered to create these theories based on similar perspectives. These personality theories are:

Type Theories

As the name suggests, these theories show the perspective of how personalities can be divided into a limited number of types. The personality types are connected to biological influences.

Trait Theories

Trait theories provide a genetics-based perspective on personality. Traits that make up a personality are stable and consistent characteristics that show in most situations. States on the other hand are temporary characteristics (e.g., a state of panic). These temporary characteristics are triggered by a certain stimulus and usually just pass by. Knowing the difference between traits and states is important.

Psychodynamic Theories

Strongly influenced by the works of Sigmund Freud, psychodynamic theories emphasize the influence of our subconscious mind on personality. It means that our pattern of thinking and behavior is mainly driven by the subconscious mind. Examples of psychodynamic theories include Freud's Psychosexual Stage Theory and Erik Erikson's Stages of Psychosocial Development.

Behavioral Theories

Behavioral theorists believe that a person's personality is shaped by his interaction with his environment. These theories focus on observable and measurable behaviors of an individual, looking past the role of internal thoughts and feelings.

Humanist Theories

Humanist Theorists believe that an individual's free will is the major source of how a personality is formed. Coupled with different life experiences as an individual grows up, it is believed that we form our personality through thoughts and actions that we decide for ourselves. This perspective is much more open to different possibilities and variables that can develop a personality. Carl Rogers and Abraham Maslow were humanist theorists.

Philosophical Assumptions on Personality[4]

Besides the different perspectives on psychology, it is equally important to equip ourselves with knowledge on some of the philosophical assumptions on personality. This will allow us to see personality through a wider lens. Some of these philosophical assumptions are:

1. **Heredity vs. Environment:** Are you familiar with the nature vs. nurture debate? This debate includes questions of whether or not something is brought

about by biological or social processes. There are many arguments about personality being a natural, biologically coded part of a newborn or being a development process as a person grows. Modern theorists like Robert Cloninger, however, believe that personality is both a biological and social attribute.

2. **Freedom vs. Determinism:** While some people believe that personality is a built-in feature which we have no control over, there are also those who believe that an individual's free will can govern his personality. This means that instead of looking at personality as an uncontrollable force, we have the freedom to form and even change it.

3. **Optimistic vs. Pessimistic:** The optimistic–pessimistic dichotomy suggests that optimistic people believe that their personality can be improved. Pessimistic people on the other hand are often seen as stubborn and unwilling to change. However, it is not because they outright reject the idea of personality development. Often, it is because they think that changing their personalities can bring even worse outcomes.

4. **Uniqueness vs. Universality:** Theorists such as Abraham Maslow believe that humans are unique to each other. We have different sets of characteristics which makes us behave, think, and feel differently from each other. Behaviorists and cognitive theorists

like Jean Piaget argue that all of us possess the same universal nature.
5. **Active vs. Reactive:** Some cognitive theorists believe that humans are active agents of their actions. We decide what we do, and we follow an internal process. Behaviorists believe that humans are reactive to whatever happens around them. This means that everything we do is just a reaction to an external force.

Can Your Personality Be Changed?[5]

In the past, psychologists argued whether personality is a biological or social product (the never-ending nature vs. nurture debate). As research progressed, they are now more convinced that they are not mutually exclusive. Personality is shaped both by genetics and environment. While genetics are absolute, environment is variable.

This is why psychologists like Carol Dweck believe that personality can be changed to a certain degree. These traits are what she calls the *in-between traits*. Belief systems, goals, and coping strategies are some examples of such in-between traits. These are the minor traits found on top of your broad traits—the grounded, untouchable ones.[6]

When a person changes his belief system (e.g. philosophy, religion) it can greatly affect his overall pattern of thinking and emotions. The same goes with changing your goals in life and the strategies you use to cope with stress. When you change these things, your mind and body will follow over time. Thus, your personality gets altered as a consequence.

Earlier in this chapter we have discussed that personality is stable over time. However, due to an ever-changing environment, there are some traits on the surface that can be altered.

Can a person who has issues with her personality change it? How?

Jumping from one personality type to another can seem implausible, but it is doable to a certain extent. First, you need to focus on changing your habits. Since habits are learned, training yourself to doing something can eventually change your personality. This includes your habitual responses, mechanisms, and coping strategies.

Focus on the process. Acknowledge your efforts, don't get discouraged if some of your abilities slow the process down. Be aware of your areas of improvement. Focus on your growth.

Remember, no matter how hard it may be, improving yourself is always a worthwhile journey. If you really want to change your personality for the better, distinguish the *in-between traits* from your *broad traits* and see how you can refine the former. Your efforts can eventually result in smarter decisions, better relationships, and an overall improved life quality.

3
Freud vs. Jung

Sigmund Freud

Sigmund Freud is a household name in the field of psychology. Freud is an Austrian neurologist and is the founder of psychoanalysis. Psychoanalysis is a clinical method of treating psychopathology through dialogues where a psychoanalyst regularly talks with his patient. Up until this day, this approach has influenced various clinical practices in psychology, and psychiatry.

Most of Freud's works are heavily influenced by his belief that underneath the mantle of our words and expressions, there lies mental processes hidden to the conscious mind. He believed that adults are strongly influenced by their childhood experiences. For instance, a person who has a traumatic childhood experience may exhibit anxiety-driven behaviors and thoughts caused by the trauma—unbeknownst to him.

Freud spent most of his time studying and attempting to penetrate the barrier between the conscious and unconscious mind. His studies explored how this barrier hides the real motivation for human behavior and psychology. His works are widely known, making his lexicon embedded in the field of psychology. Some of the words he introduced are libido, neurotic, Freudian slip and cathartic.

The Unconscious Mind[1]

Using the image of an iceberg, Freud developed a topographical model of the mind that presents its three levels. These levels include characteristics of the mind's structure, and function. The tip of the iceberg represents the consciousness which consist of our present thoughts. Present thoughts mean the things we focus our attention to at the moment.

Just below the tip is the preconscious. This consists of everything that our memory can retrieve. Lastly, in Freud's studies the most significant region, is the unconscious. This is where the real motivations of our behavior sit. Just like an iceberg, this most important part of our mind is of which we cannot see.

The unconscious mind is like a storage where all our deepest desires, impulses but also painful and frightening memories are kept. Some experiences can be so traumatic that they get locked up in the unconscious mind. Our traumas and primitive wishes are then mediated by the preconscious.

Freud used this theory to experience with his patients. He observed that most of his patients have a hard time describing frightening or painful experiences. He believed that it is because the information relating to these events are locked in the unconscious mind through repression. Under this assumption, he theorized that the unconscious mind takes a bigger control of human behavior more than we could ever know. His goal was to make the unconscious mind, conscious.

The Id, Ego, and Superego[2]

In 1923, Freud was able to develop the model of three levels of mind into the three 'psychic apparatus' namely id, ego, and superego. These are not actual areas of the brain, but rather conceptualizations of important mental functions. The three concepts, id, ego, and superego, are the three key components of someone's personality according to Freud.

Freud believed that the id sits at the unconscious level and works to gratify the basic human needs. Id consists of two biological instincts which he called Eros and Thanatos. Eros is the life instinct while Thanatos is the death instinct. Eros directs basic survival activities like breathing, eating, and reproduction. Thanatos on the other hand is believed to be a set destructive forces in humans and it manifests as aggression and violence. As Eros is stronger than Thanatos, human race survives instead of self-destruct.

Ego develops during infancy. Ego serves as an enabler of what the id wants. However, ego finds a way to satisfy the id's desires in a socially acceptable way. Ego operates both at the conscious and unconscious levels.

Lastly, superego develops during early childhood. Superego serves as our moral compass. It makes us act and behave based on morality and the principles accepted in the environment we live in.

Because the id, ego, and superego function differently from each other, a conflict often ensues when there is a desire which cannot be morally gratified. One example of this incompatibility is when the id expresses a desire that the superego deems socially unacceptable. The superego can make us feel guilty for wanting such thing.

An imbalance among the three can make up an extreme personality. A person with an overly dominant id can be impulsive, stubborn, or even violent. An overly dominant ego might mean rigidness in personality. Someone who has overly dominant superego might become a very self-righteous person. He also has the tendency to be judgmental of others' shortcomings.

Because imbalances and inner conflicts occur, Freud believes that a person should have an ego strength. This means that the ego should be able to deal with the other two components and find a dynamic balance. Thus the person should also be able to function despite the conflicting forces of the three.

Defense Mechanisms[3]

When things become too overwhelming, the ego deploys various defense mechanisms. These defense mechanisms work at the unconscious level and help the ego fight unpleasant feelings like anxiety. Anxiety usually happens when there is a desire that in in conflict issues with an individual's moral value, self-esteem, or worldview.

What are the different defense mechanisms?

Repression

The first defense mechanism that Freud discovered was repression. Repression is the act of warding off thoughts and preventing it from becoming conscious. While it can be a great band-aid solution, this approach is not successful in the long run. Repressing your thoughts and desires could only lead to anxiety because you are forcing them into the unconscious. Them being hidden does not mean they will not resurface later on.

Projection

Projection is attributing your own thoughts and feelings to another person. Because you cannot accept these thoughts or desires, you force them onto other people. Common examples of these thoughts are violence and sexual desires which often cause guilt to some people. A might want to punch B in the face but A's superego knows that's not the right thing to do, thus A convinces him or herself that B wants to punch him or her in the face. Thus A justifies his or her own feelings being right.

Displacement

Displacement is redirection of your impulse to an often more powerless substitute target. This target can be a person or an object. For example, when you are frustrated and start throwing random things, that is a displacement of your emotions. You are taking out your anger on something else.

Sublimation

The difference between displacement and sublimation is that sublimation means taking out our emotions in a constructive way rather than choosing the destructive route. Sublimation can be largely seen with artistic people. When they feel hurt or frustrated, you can see them turning to music or painting. Sport is another way of letting out aggression in a productive way.

Denial

Anna Freud (1936) believed that denial is one defense mechanism wherein we intentionally refuse awareness of something. When a situation gets too stressful, we instantly block them from our consciousness. This mechanism can operate by itself or side by side another defense mechanism. However, it is undeniably a futile defense mechanism as any prerogative to disregard reality is a harmful behavior.

Regression

Have you ever experienced such tremendous stress that you just became childish (e.g. making faces, heckling, etc.)? This is what we call regression. When we are faced with extreme stress, our behavior can become more childish or even primitive. This can happen intentionally or unintentionally. Another example is when a ten-year-old boy wets his bed (just like when he was younger) because he is nervous or afraid.

Criticisms on Freud

While it is undeniable that Freud had a great impact in the field of psychology and human development, his work also got a lot of criticism. During his time, many people were skeptic of his theories because they are neither provable or refutable. His theory was viewed as highly unscientific because his parameters couldn't be tested or measured objectively. For example, how do you test or measure the unconcious mind?

Additionally, Freudian psychology did not have enough evidence to support claims. Freud mostly studied himself, his patients, and his child. His case studies were not representative as the size of the sample was small. His methodology was also very much susceptible to bias in his interpretations.

Despite these criticisms, Freud believed that qualitative differences among people are more valuable factors to observe.

He stood by his theory and believed that his findings still held significance in the field of psychology. His theories are influencial on modern psychology researches up until this day.

Carl Jung[4]

Carl Gustav Jung is known as the Father of Analytic (Jungian) Psychology. While this school of thought shares a lot of similarities with Freud's psychoanalytic method such as the importance of the unconscious, Jung believed in different facets on how it works and develops human psychology. Theoretical differences led them to go their separate ways. Jung went on and developed his own version of psychoanalytic theories. In 1912, Jung even criticized Freud's theory of the Oedipus complex while on a lecture in America.

While Jung agreed with Freud that childhood experiences heavily influence our behavior in adulthood, he also believed that we are also motivated and defined by our future aspirations. In developing a theory of personality, he came out with eight different types of personality based on introversion and extroversion. He also identified four functions that personality has: feeling, thinking, sensation, and intuition.

Feeling and thinking belong to rational thought processes where we consciously define the value and meaning of something. Sensation and intuition on the other hand are non-rational thought processes as they are mainly based on our senses and initial feelings. These cognitive functions are what he called the rational (judging) function and the irrational (perceiving) function.

Jung believed that each of the functions are reflected either in an introverted or extraverted attitude. Combining these functions with these two attitudes, Jung was able to form the eight types of personality:

1. extroverted-thinking
2. introverted-thinking
3. extroverted-feeling
4. introverted-feeling
5. extroverted-sensing
6. introverted-sensing
7. extroverted-intuitive
8. introverted-intuitive

Jung's personality types became the basis of the Myers-Briggs Type Indicator (MBTI). MBTI is the number one personality assessment tool used to determine how a person perceives the world and makes decisions.[5]

Myers-Briggs Type Indicator® (MBTI®)[6]

While Jung's work is the foundation of the MBTI, it's important to note that MBTI employed a different approach. The purpose of the MBTI is to expand Jung's personality theory in a way that people will understand and find useful. They also wanted to create an inventory of personality types which are based on a much more controlled and scientific personality assessment. This is in contrary to Jung's psychoanalysis method of anecdotes and observations, which are deemed inconclusive.

The MBTI took the route of a 'structured' approach instead of the 'projective' approach employed by Jung. In a structured approach, personality assessment is based on 'closed' items which are solely interpreted according to the theory of the test constructors in scoring. In contrast, a projective approach uses 'open-ended' responses which are contextual and susceptible to interpretation bias.

Myers and Briggs did not confine themselves with Jung's studies on personality. They added their own concepts to it such as the extraverted functions of Judging (J) or Perceiving (P) which act as the fourth letter in an MBTI personality type. Myers and Briggs believe that extraverts either have J or P as their dominant function while introverts have J or P as their auxiliary function. This dichotomy will be further explained in the next section.

The Four Dichotomies[7]

Jung believed that people are either born with or can develop a certain way of perceiving and deciding. These psychological differences are reflected in the MBTI with its four dichotomies or the four opposite pairs. These are the four consecutive letters that you will see in each personality type such as I-N-F-P.

1. **The Extravert–Introvert Dichotomy:** Being an extravert or an introvert is considered a person's attitude. Extraverts (E-type) are outgoing, energetic and active. They often get their motivation from external forces and can easily express themselves. Introvert (I-type) people can be timid, reserved, and value their privacy a lot. While they can be deemed as shy, this is not always the case. They just prefer thinking on their own and do not draw energy from people around them.

   Extraverts don't have a hard time creating relationships. Their highly communicative tendencies can win them a lot of friends. They prefer working in a team than working alone. However, extreme extraversion can be bothersome for a few people. Their high energy, cheerfulness, and even clinginess could be a problem short and long-term interactions.

   Introverts on the other hand take time in letting people in. Since they get energy and information from internal sources, they do not see as much need to gain a lot of friends. Their silent withdrawal can come off as rude to some people. They may also seem bored and disinterested when in a crowd. But this couldn't be further from the truth. It's just a sign of internal thought processing.

2. **The Sensing–Intuition Dichotomy:** When we gather information, we use our sensing and intuition. People who prefer to use their senses are more likely to trust the information at hand. They prefer when information is

tangible and concrete—easy for the five senses to digest. Intuitive people like to associate information with other established information. They seek wider context and patterns and add their own interpretations to them.

Sensors (S-type) are practical people. What you see is what you get. They are more comfortable with things that are measurable and empirical. Intuitives (N-type) are more imaginative. They like making predictions and focusing on the future.

3. **The Feeling–Thinking Dichotomy:** Our two judging functions come from thinking and feeling. Both of these functions are used to make rational decisions based on the information received from the information-collecting functions, sensing and intuition. People who prefer to use their thinking function tend to look at the bigger picture. They weigh in consequences, think of logical and reasonable causes and consequences, and follow a certain set of rules.

Those who prefer feeling on the other hand are more empathizing. They put themselves in other people's shoes just so they can get a better grasp of the situation. They also consider the needs of every party involved. Their decisions are usually instinct-based.

Thinkers (T-type) are big on logic. They do not let their personal emotions or prejudice get in the way when making a decision. They use their heads over their hearts. Feelers (F-type) are emotional people and can easily associate with others. Their feelings play a major role when they make a decision because they fear getting hurt or worse, hurting other people.

4. **The Judging–Perceiving Dichotomy:** The last dichotomy indicates the dominant extraverted function of an individual. Jung believed that while we use all four cognitive functions (sensing, intuition, thinking, and feeling), one function is always predominantly used. After the dominant function comes the auxiliary function, and to a lesser degree, the tertiary function. The least conscious function is what Myers called the 'shadow.' Each function is applied in either introverted or extraverted manner. Someone who has extraverted sensing, for instance, uses sensing differently than someone who has introverted sensing as a dominant function.

   Myers and Briggs added the J or P dichotomy to show that people also have a preference between judging or perceiving. If you have taken the MBTI before, you will notice that a personality type ends with either J or P. These letters indicate the most preferred extraverted function (judgment/perception) of a person. For extroverts, this is their dominant function and for introverts, this is their auxiliary function. For example, for ENFP people, perceiving is their dominant function. For an INFP, it is just their auxiliary function.

   People who have strong judging function (J-type) like having things organized and clear. They prefer planning ahead of time. By having order and control, they can make quick and better decisions. Perceivers (P-type) live in spontaneity. They do not like structure and feel uncomfortable when something is too controlled. They love having freedom and flexibility.

Furthermore, judging types can be divided into categories: Thinking-Judging (TJ) types and Feeling-Judging (FJ) types. TJ people depend on logic and reason while FJ types use their emotions and compassion more when judging. For perceptive types we have Sensing-Perceiving (SP) and Intuition-Perceiving (NP). SP types are concrete while NP types tend to see the world as abstract or ideal.

Criticisms on the MBTI

MBTI questionnaires are deemed too general and ambiguous. Its precision is questioned because items apply to a variety of situations and behaviors. Test takers are also guillable to give a high rating to a positive description which they would like to apply to them. There are no validity scales to screen responses which can be exaggerated or made socially fitting.

The test-retest reliability of MBTI also shows a low percentage of accuracy. Majority of the people who did a retake of the test got different personality types even if the tests were just done weeks apart. However, MBTI said that accurate results of the test solely depends on the test taker's honesty. MBTI also made it clear that their test is just a basis of personality type assessment. It should never be used as an official psychological test.[8]

Would You Like to Take the MBTI Test?

If you would like to have an idea about your personality type, you can trust that the MBTI will give you a strong basis to work with. If you are just taking the test for fun, you can head on over to https://www.16personalities.com to take the test for free. If you want more exhaustive explanations for your test score, you can take the test for $49 here: https://www.mbtionline.com/TaketheMBTI.

You can use your results here as a basis for a perfect job fit for you or even for choosing dating partners. Just remember that the MBTI test only aims to provide a personality framework, not 100 percent accurate result.

4

Gary Chapman's Languages

Gary Chapman, the writer of the book *The 5 Love Languages* and an American family counselor, has conducted more than thirty years of research on this particular topic, which resulted in determining and describing five ways to express and experience love: receiving gifts, quality time, words of affirmation, acts of service, and physical touch.[1]

Chapman states that every single person has a primary love language; like his or her love language mother tongue, the language through which he or she feels loved the most. It's no use for an American to try to talk to a German if they can't speak the other's language. The same applies to the love language exchange. Expecting someone to feel truly loved by 'speaking' to her via a different love language is the same as expecting a German to understand English. Quite simply, they are unable to communicate with each other.

To ensure proper communication and full understanding of each other, Chapman encourages to learn the other's love language and decode the various ways in which couples communicate with one another, or generally how people interact, so we can finally understand what our significant other really wants from us.

In the following section I will invite you to learn about the preferences of others when it comes to receiving love. The rules apply to family relations, romantic relationships, and workplace relations as well. You can deal with other people better if you know their love language.

Chapman suggests that in order to identify someone's love language, one must carefully observe:

- the way person in question expresses love;
- analyze what he or she complains about the most;
- what does he or she request from their significant other most frequently.

According to Chapman's hypothesis, people tend to instinctively give love in the way that they wish to receive it. Better communication, deeper intimacy between couples can be fostered when one can show caring to the other in the love language the recipient understands.

For example, a husband may be confused and feel unappreciated when he does the dishes for his wife and she doesn't seem to express genuine gratitude and feelings of being loved. She may see the dishwashing, as a chore that must be done thus doing it doesn't mean a thing. The wife's dominant love language may be physical touch thus she could understand and appreciate her husband's love better through a tight embrace or a relaxing neck massage. She may try to express love to her husband based on what she values, physical touch, but he may not value it as much as she does. If the wife understands that his love language is acts of service and washes the car for him, he would perceive it as a genuine act of expressing her love for him. Similarly, if he cuddles up to her in the bed after dinner, she will value that as a deep act of love.

Most importantly, you should discover and understand your own love language first. Why is this important? Maybe you could never articulate what exactly you missed in your relationship, but you often felt your 'love tank' was empty. With the help of the love languages you can tell your partner, your mother, or your friend how can they make you feel truly appreciated.

What's your love language? Find out by completing Gary Chapman's love language test at www.5lovelanguages.com. After you're done with the completion of the test, ask your partner, friends and family to complete it, as well. Make a note of the results of your loved ones and consciously commit to practice showing love on their primary love language.

Keep in mind that just because you and your partner have a dominant love language doesn't mean you should stop 'using' the other love languages. If strawberry is your favorite fruit, it doesn't mean you wouldn't eat an apple from time to time. The same goes for having different dominant love languages. Just because your primary love language is physical touch and your partner's acts of service it doesn't mean that you're a bad match for each other. It only means you prefer strawberry and he loves apples.

Words of Affirmation

As one famous song goes, *words can heal a thousand souls*. This is definitely true for people who have words of affirmation as their primary love language. These people prefer hearing compliments and verbal expression of emotions. They feel secure when the people around them tell them that they are important or that they are loved. Words of appreciation and even terms of endearment are very effective love communicators for these people.

As much as words of encouragement affect them, saying negative things or unpleasant words to them can hit them hard. Holding grudges can be a common thing for them especially if the words really hurt. Harsh words are not easily forgiven, even more so forgotten.

Just like real languages, Dr. Chapman believes that love languages also have their dialects. In the case of words of affirmation, its dialects are encouraging words, kind words, and humble words.[2]

Encouraging Words

Words of encouragement—especially from the people we love—can really turn our bad days around. Encouraging words do not intend to nag or pressure a partner. They are meant to give your partner a little push in times of self-doubt or weakness. Empathy and gentleness are much needed for your encouraging words not to sound offensive.

For an instance, you might think that you are encouraging your child to study harder by saying things like *'I know you can be the top student in your class!'* or *'100 percent is not that difficult to get if you focus hard enough.'* These words may be burdensome for students instead of encouraging. You might be implying that the only way to be a good student is to always get perfect grades.

Instead of pressuring them with words like these, you might want to try a lighter approach. Tell them that they have to work hard in school but at the same time assure them that is okay to fail from time to time. Encouragement can also come from words of comfort. By comforting them, they get more strength to go on and try even harder the next time.

If you identify yourself as a person who often needs words of encouragement, do not hesitate to express this desire to your partner. Let them know how encouraging words affect your productivity and your overall motivation. Of course, it will be difficult to always hear the words you want to hear, but you can kindly ask your partner to practice the dialect of encouraging words for you.

Kind Words

Kind words can express two things: love and pain. Tender words can reflect how a person genuinely feels. When you love a person, it is second nature for you to always say kind words to him. Not only do you use positive words, you also make sure that your feelings are conveyed by the way you talk. Kind words are complemented by tone, facial expression and gestures.

On the other hand, you can also express your pain through kind words. If your partner did something offensive, you can always say *'I honestly felt bad when you…'* or *'Let's work on what happened earlier. I want you to know that it hurt me.'* If we wrap our pain in such gentle words, it will most likely yield favorable results of reconciliation. Asking for forgiveness is also easier when you use the dialect of kind words.

Humble Words

There is a thin line between requesting and demanding. We all have the tendency to sound rude and demanding when expressing what we want. By using humble words, we can request for things without coming off as bossy. For example, instead of straight out saying *'You've been too busy lately. I want us to go on a trip this summer'*, you can say *'I think going on a vacation is a good way to spend our summer together, do you want to do that?'*

Quality Time

Presence is the main theme of this love language. Quality time means being there for your partner and giving them your undivided attention. For people whose love language is quality time, it is very important to feel your genuine presence in their lives. Texting or calling can give them good vibes when you're apart but when you're physically close they need you to be there.

Broken promises are a big no to these people. Postponed dates or even being late can seem as neglect. They do not appreciate you being constantly on your phone when you are with them. They want you to give them your time and attention because they are willing to give you just as much. Expression of this love language can go from simple movie nights to vacation trips or other outdoor activities.

Quality Conversations

To have quality time is also to have quality conversations. Quality conversations happen when both of you fully exchange thoughts and experiences. You are not only physically present, but you are an active contributor to the conversation. For quality conversations to happen, a relationship must have trust, honesty, and a certain level of comfortability.

Quality conversations are on dialect of the quality time love language. Dr. Chapman believes that quality conversations can only be attained when people do these five things: eye contact, giving undivided attention, listening for feelings, paying attention to body language, and avoiding interruptions.

When having a conversation with your partner, maintaining eye contact is important. It reflects how interested you are with what they are saying. Furthermore, giving your undivided attention entails not doing anything while the both of you are talking. Your partner might find it rude when you keep fiddling on your phone or watching the TV while they are pouring their heart out.

Listening to your partner's feelings means that you make yourself aware of their emotions while speaking. Paying attention to how they sound like will give you an idea if they feel upset or excited. Their body language is also another reflection of how they truly feel. You should familiarize yourself with your partner's body signals of fear or anger. They can be seen from trembling, teary eyes or clenching of fists among others.

Lastly, avoid interrupting your partner when speaking. Listen intently and make them feel that they can tell you anything that they desire. Even when having an argument, restrain yourself from butting in. Make a mental note of your partner's points and respond only when they are done. Facilitate a two-way conversation.

Quality Activities

Another dialect of quality time is quality activity. Quality activities can be anything that either one of you or the both of you are interested in. The purpose of these quality activities is for the both you to share great experiences and create a stronger bond. These activities will deepen your relationship's intimacy.

Love is especially expressed when you are willing to engage in activities you are not interested in just because your partner wants it. When your boyfriend agrees to watch sloppy dramas with you or waits in line with you as you get that lipstick you've been eyeing, it is one proof that he is willing to spend quality time with you, no matter what activity it might be.

Receiving Gifts

There are people whose love language is receiving tangible gifts. They are not materialistic, they just want something to remember a person by. The act of gift-giving is a reminder for them that they are appreciated and loved. Most of the time, it is not the gift itself that they are most thankful for, but the time and effort spent by their partner.

How can you express love in this language? Gift-giving is a complex act of love. It depends on different variables like budget and individual preferences. Nevertheless, it is important to note that giving a gift is not an act to flaunt wealth but rather an act to express love. Your thoughtfulness carries the real value of the gift and not its price.

Ultimately, be reminded that gifts do not always have to be material or pricey things. Why don't you try other gifts like cooking dinner for your partner or even writing her a song? Expressing love in this language will surely test your creative ideas!

Acts of Service

For people who have acts of service as their main language of love, it is very important that you always act upon your words. Talk means nothing to them if you don't follow up with your actions. For these people, they feel their value when their partner, family or friends go out of their way to help them.

Showing your love to these people mean that you are willing to do favors for them. May it be household chores or helping them out on their work, what matters is that they see you're making an effort to make things easier for them. They feel secured in the fact that they have a partner in you.

Now, how can you offer acts of service without making your partner become too dependent on you? The answer is to create a boundary through conditions. Do not just say yes to every request, let your partner know your limitations. Avoid the occurrence of emotional manipulation by making it clear that you have the power to decide which requests you grant and which you think are out of your capacity. As Chapman says, allowing yourself to be used is not an act of love but an act of treason.

To speak this love language more efficiently, you and your partner should take the time to evaluate your roles in the relationship. Moreover, it is equally necessary that you discuss the society's stereotypes of gender roles and how they play in your relationship. It is important that you discuss these stereotypes with a progressive mindset.

Physical Touch

For people whose love language is physical touch, physical connections are the most important. They feel loved and secure when you hold their hands, hug them or kiss them. For women, they feel safe when their man's arms are around them. This gesture can be perceived as an act of protection.

Physical touch is a powerful tool to express your love. It can go from simple hand-holding to much more intimate acts like sexual intercourse. As the relationship grows deeper, physical connection also becomes more intimate and more prominent.

Showing your love through this language can be tricky. There are physical touches which are deemed appropriate and inappropriate. What's important is that you openly discuss intimacy with your partner. Consent is the key to expressing this love language more effectively. Both parties in a relationship should be aware of their boundaries.

Understanding Your Own Love Language

It is very important that you are aware of your own love language. Familiarizing yourself with your emotional needs will help you and your partner to cultivate a deeper relationship. To get an idea of your primary and even your secondary love language, you can start by asking yourself these questions:

What do I usually request from my partner, family, or friends?
What makes me feel happy?
How do I approach relationship problems?
Am I the expressive or the reserved type?
What makes me feel loved the most?

Your answers will serve as your guide in finding out what your love language is. Whether you value words, quality time or physical contact, it is necessary that you are in touch with your subconscious desires. Not only will you be able to express them to your partner, but you can also identify areas of improvement. If you feel neglected because your partner might have not expressed his love through your language, you can easily explain to them.

Know that when you have unmet needs, this can pave the way for a failed relationship. If the both of you do not discuss what you want, an emotional gap is bound to happen. It can start gradually, like distancing yourselves or putting a wall against each other. As time passes by, you will realize that the longer you keep your desires to yourselves, the wider your distance becomes.

The Five Apology Languages[3]

Forgiving and asking for forgiveness can be two of the toughest things to do in the world. Saying sorry is never easy. And even if an apology has been uttered, sometimes it is not enough.

In any type of relationship, humility and maturity can go a long way. Admitting that you are wrong and genuinely making up for it are very important things to do when hurtful incidents happen. In order to move forward from any relationship hurdles, there are five apology languages that people commonly subscribe to. Gary Chapman and Jennifer Thomas identified them as:

Making Restitution

Rectification is the key in this apology language. If you did something wrong, you have to make an effort of straightening them out. For people who have restitution as their apology language, it is important for them to see that you are trying to make things right again. You can't just leave your mess or cover it up with words.

In order to express your apology, you must first know what your partner's love language is. Making amends can mean spending more time with your partner, being more intimate or giving them gifts. A sincere apology for these people means that you assure them that you love them, and you accompany that assurance with actions.

Accepting Responsibility

Admission of any wrongdoing is often a tough call. To say that something is our fault is equivalent to saying that we failed.

However, no matter how hard it can be, it is important that we all learn how to be accountable for our actions. People who seek taking responsibility as their apology language look for humility from their partners. They want to hear an apology where their partner admits that they were wrong.

If there is denial or resistance, an apology might not be accepted by these people. It is important for them that their partners are willing to let go of their ego and accept their time of weakness. Additionally, they want the full truth when you explain yourselves to them. They will not accept a half-baked apology.

People with this apology language appreciate it when you show your vulnerability to them. They perceive this act as trust. When you wholeheartedly say that you made a mistake and apologize for it, it becomes so much easier for them to forgive.

Expressing Regret

This apology language focuses on feelings of guilt and shame. People who speak this language need to be assured that you regret hurting them. Most of the time, your expression of guilt and regret is already enough for them. They usually do not expect you to make any amends aside from your sincere apology.

Expressing regret is one of the easiest apology languages to 'speak' because it is simple and straightforward. It does not need any other things except your remorse. If your partner speaks this apology language, you can expect that they only need you to make them feel that you are not proud of what you did to them.

Since expressing regret is more of a verbal act, it is important to accompany it with sincere actions. It can be reflected through your body language and the way you act or talk to them after the incident. Sincerity is often mirrored through a person's eye contact, gentle words and sometimes, even tears.

Genuinely Repenting

Genuinely repenting is all about change. People who speak this apology language will only consider an apology if you also express your desire to change. It is important for them that you are aware of what you did wrong and which unhealthy behavior you need to work on.

Repentance is an intrinsic process. It all begins within you. While your partner can help point out what needs to be changed, you must also know your own bad habits. In a healthy relationship, one must be willing to modify himself so that he can be a better partner. This is not to strip you off your self-identity but rather to mold you into the type of person who considers his partner's needs.

Repenting can be a difficult journey. It entails a lot of changing. If you want your apology to be successful, you must first make a realistic set of goals. What are the changes that you need to achieve? List them down. After that, take baby steps to work towards your goals. It can be hard from time to time, but keep in mind that if you genuinely want to repent, you have to pull through and change for the better.

Requesting Forgiveness

Some people want to hear their partners ask for forgiveness. It is not arrogance but the natural need to be assured that their partner knows that forgiveness is needed. When their partner asks for forgiveness, it makes them feel that their partners truly want to restore their relationship.

When you ask for forgiveness, you acknowledge the fact that your offended partner has the upper hand in the situation. They have the right to choose to forgive you or not. Asking for forgiveness is different from demanding it. You have to leave the decision up to them and respect whatever it may be.

Why is asking for forgiveness a difficult thing for people? Because we fear rejection. When we realize that we did something wrong, we can only hope that the other person will give us a chance to make things right again. However, we all know that not everybody gets a second chance. This fear can often hinder us from asking for forgiveness.

Usually, a heartfelt apology gets forgiveness. Sincerity is the key. Your partner needs to feel that you know you are at fault and that you are willing to make up for it. When you are given forgiveness, do not take it for granted. Show your partner that you are grateful for it. You can thank them through their love language.

Chapman and Thomas point out on two key aspects of human fulfillment in their books, namely how to love and be loved in a fulfilling way and how to restore damaged relationships in a healthy way. Knowing what we love and what the people closest to us love is crucial to be able to communicate what we need from them and to give the best we can to them. It is equally important to know how to make things right when we make a mistake—voluntarily or by accident. We are humans, we err, and that's okay. The problem arises when we don't realize how we hurt another human being with our actions, we fail to apologize and take responsibility for our actions. The less accountable we are for our actions, the more people will eventually draw away from us.

We talked about the importance of human connection we seek so badly—understanding how to love and how to apologize can improve our social life enormously. These two life-skills are the entrance ticket to good relationships.

5
Temperament Types

Temperament is an individual's way of thinking, behaving, or reacting. It is a series of inborn traits which cause us to act the way we do. Coming from the Latin word *temperamentum* which means right blending, ancient historians believed that a person's temperament is made up of body fluids blending with each other.

Origin[1][2]

Greek historian Hippocrates (460–370 BC) is one of the pioneers who studied the human's temperament. He believed that a person's behavior is caused by body fluids called humors. He identified these humors as red bile or blood (sanguis), yellow bile (cholera), black bile (melas) and white bile or phlegm. Later on, Greek physician Galen (131–200 AD) developed his own typology of temperament as he sought for the different physiological reasons behind a person's behavior.

An excess of blood or red bile is believed to result to a sanguine temperament which is warm (hot and wet) and is associated with the element of air. Another warm (hot and dry) temperament is choleric which is an excess of the yellow bile. It is associated with the element of fire.

Cool temperaments are caused by black and white bile. An excess of white bile results to a cool (cold and wet) temperament which is associated with the element of water. It is called the phlegmatic temperament. Lastly, melancholic temperament is an excess of the black bile. It is a cool (cold and dry) temperament and is associated with the element of earth.

The theory of temperaments was then expanded by Persian polymath Avicenna (980–1037) to encompass psychological aspects such as emotions, mental capacity, morality, and dreams. He believed that the human behavior is beyond physiological reasons. However, English physician Nicholas Culpeper altogether rejected the idea that temperaments are physiological or motivated by body fluids. Other scientists that are major contributors on the modern temperament theories are Alfred Adler, Maimonides, Immanuel Kant, and Ivan Pavlov.

Hans Eysenck is known as one of the first psychologists who used psycho-statistical analysis to study personality differences. Upon research, he believed that temperament is biological. In his book *Dimensions of Personality*, he presented two dimensions of personality: neuroticism and extraversion. He believed that neuroticism (N) is the tendency to feel negative emotions while extraversion (E) is savoring positive moments which are usually social events.

Eysenck observed that when two dimensions were paired, the results were the same as the four temperaments identified by ancient historians. From here on, various systems were developed by researchers to identify temperaments. Most of these researchers opted not to use the ancient temperament names.

Keirsey Temperament Sorter (KTS) is one of the most popular system nowadays. This questionnaire is widely used to help people assess themselves and better understand their personality traits. The four temperaments of Keirsey Temperament Sorter are based on the Greek gods Apollo, Dionysus, Epimetheus and Prometheus. They are also heavily influenced by the sixteen types of personality from the Myers-Briggs Type Indicator (MBTI).

KTS' four temperaments are: Artisan (SP), Guardian (SJ), Idealist (NF), and Rational (NT). Instead of using the dichotomy of extraversion and introversion, the KTS paired Sensing and Intuition (which they renamed as Concrete and Abstract) to a new category: Cooperative and Pragmatic. Factoring in Role-Informativeness and Role Directiveness which correspond to orientation to people or task, the sixteen types are formed.

What Is and What Isn't Temperament?[3]

As mentioned, temperament is a cluster of inborn traits which cause you to behave in a certain way. It is not a personality type nor a reflection of character. We say that temperaments are traits rather than types because the trait approach leaves a room for varying degrees of expression or development. On the other hand, the type approach is absolute and rather restrictive. It is a strict category which a person may fit or not fit in. As psychologist Gordon Allport said, a man can be said to have a trait, but he cannot be said to have a type, rather, he fits a type.[4]

A cluster of traits result to a specific human behavior. These traits or tendencies vary from low to high expression. The degree of these tendencies determines the temperament a person may have. For example, the warm temperaments (Choleric and Sanguine) express certain tendencies on a comparable degree which makes them similar to each other yet different from those with cool temperaments (Phlegmatic and Melancholy).

Temperament reflects the reactive process of individuals. It shows how we respond or relate to different situations. Temperament is said to be predictable as you can base the temperament traits on the stimulus present. Most of the time, you can predict how a person will react based on the situation you are witnessing. However, in times wherein a person experiences strong emotion such as anger, frustration or fear, the temperament traits can come unpredictably. Intentional deception is also make it hard to guess someone's temperament.

Moreover, temperament is a force. It produces an urge that needs to be satisfied. A person's temperament can drive him to behave in a particular manner. For example, people who are shy and enjoy their privacy are driven by the desire of solitude. This internal force causes them to avoid contact with people they are not comfortable with and drives them to satisfy the urge of having their time all to themselves. A person's traits or tendencies naturally come out when a temperament needs to be satisfied.

Lastly, temperament is a need. As you have read, temperament needs to be satisfied. It is a desire that an individual needs to fill. When an individual's temperament is not acted upon, it causes a person to feel some void. A person will continue to feel unwell until his temperament is satisfied.[5]

People who have the Sanguine temperament enjoy social interactions. They feel an internal force to socialize and be around people. When they go on for too long without any social interactions, they start to feel bored and later on feel restless. They will naturally seek for ways to fill the void and behave in a way which will lead them to satisfy their need of conversing with people.

The Four Temperaments[6]

From Galen's own typology of temperament, it is observed that pairs of warm and cool temperaments share similar traits.

Warm Temperaments

Sanguine (hot/wet) and choleric (hot/dry) temperaments share the trait of quickness of response. People with sanguine temperament are usually impulsive, have fast but short-lived reactions. Choleric temperament on the other hand also cause people to respond quickly but their responses are sustained for a relatively longer time.

Cool Temperaments

Conversely, phlegmatic (cold/wet) and melancholic (cold/dry) temperaments both share the trait of a longer response. While both phlegmatic and melancholic temperaments have a longer response-delay, phlegmatic exhibit short-lived responses while melancholic temperament exhibit responses which are usually long-term, if not permanent.

Other similarity to note is of that between warm choleric and cool melancholy. As you can observe, both temperaments hold responses for a long period of time. This means that people with these temperaments often hold on to emotions like anger and pain. This can make them appear more serious. The only difference is that choleric tend to express their anger quickly while melancholic tend to keep it in and unintentionally create pent up emotions.

Among these four temperaments, melancholy and sanguine would be the opposites, as choleric and phlegmatic are.

What Drives These Four Temperaments?

Because Sanguine are 'people-people', they are driven by their need for attention. They always have the urge to interact with people and be present in social events. They also have the tendency to openly accept others so that they will also be accepted. They fear rejection because it hurts their self-esteem. Impressing other people can also be one of their tendencies.

For the Melancholic, their fear of rejection is much stronger which makes it their main driving force. They also fear not knowing things or not being updated with news around them. Because they can be perfectionists, they get hurt when people tell them that they don't like their work or that it is not good enough. They love hearing compliments that is why they strive for perfection.

Life goals and dreams motivate the Choleric. Most often than not, they see connection with people as a tool that they can use to achieve these goals. Phlegmatic people on the other hand are generally laidback. Their driving need is the preservation of their energy and time.

Fundamental Concepts[7]

Before we dive in to an in-depth discussion of temperament traits, it is important to know the general keynotes of temperament. First, each individual possesses one primary and one secondary temperament. The degree of expression of the temperament traits determine which category you most likely fit in. Strengths and weaknesses are both present in all temperaments.

Traits can be developed. You can either choose to hone your natural strengths or choose to control your natural weaknesses. The development of traits depends on an individual's childhood, peers, environment, culture, education, and gender.

An individual's early home environment plays a vital role in the development of his traits. A person's self-image starts from his childhood. If an individual has a home filled with love, kindness and respect, he grows up to be a self-aware and self-fulfilled person. Our peers also affect us as we develop our traits. The people we associate with will greatly influence how we form our opinions and how we perceive the world.

Your environment, including your location and community, will mold your way of living. Your belief system will be grounded in the culture you are exposed to. The generation you belong to will also affect your values and perspective. In the same way, educational institutions you attend and the affiliations you join will offer different beliefs which you are free to subscribe to.

Lastly, the gender of an individual will motivate different needs. These biological needs will cause us to respond in specific manners to our environment.

Traits[8]

Sanguine

People with dominant sanguine temperament are generally extroverted. They enjoy social events and love being a part of the crowd. They direct their high energy on being active and social. Being people-oriented, connecting with others is a must for them. They are influenced by their peers in the same way that they have a huge influence on other people.

Individuals with this temperament do not like feeling stagnant. They are always on the go and love seeking adventures. Sanguines love to do adrenaline-inducing activities. They are outgoing and fun to be with. However, while they value companionship and camaraderie, sanguines can get very competitive.

Additionally, while they can make friends easily, they are often afraid of commitments. They can be unreliable at times. Sanguines are also known as the word smiths. They love telling stories but sometimes facts are compromised just to make the conversation exciting. They can also be very impulsive—whether it be on spending money or deciding on other important choices.

Because sanguines appear to be lacking discipline, people around them tend to remind them to be more serious and composed. They also need to be more resolute. Sanguines ought to keep in mind that some situations call for conservatism and self-control.

Choleric

The other more extroverted temperament type is the choleric. Not only do they love being in the crowd, they love leading it. They are independent and goal-oriented. They possess leadership qualities that they would like to show when they are with a group of people. While they can be ambitious, they know how to stay grounded with logic and facts.

Because cholerics can be firm, their presence can be enough for some people to feel intimidated. They can be domineering and stern especially when given the position of a leader. They do things their way and leave little to no room for negotiating. Cholerics are very much results-oriented and will not stop until they get the outcome they desire.

Peer pressure is not a problem for people with choleric temperament. They are not easily swayed. They have their own set of principles that do not waiver in any situation. This is why they are good at making decisions. They stick to what they believe is right and they do not falter. People in this group make a strong leader, boss and military officers.

However, cholerics can be very aggressive when they do not get the results they want. They tend to show their anger through shouting and even physical manifestations. They do not easily empathize with others and can come off as unfriendly and cold. They can also be unnecessarily strict and stubborn.

People with this temperament need to have more patience. Friends and family who are close to choleric often remind them to e more loving and understanding. They need to develop empathy and be less vicious to others especially people under them.

Melancholic

People under this temperament are usually deep-thinkers and feelers. They are very observant, and have a knack of noticing even the smallest of details. While they observe, they also analyze everything around them. They are self-reliant and love working alone. They do not like it when they become the center of attention. They also avoid being appointed as the group's leader.

They may not be expressive, but melancholic people know what they are doing. They are quality-oriented and operate in a plan they made for themselves. Although they keep mum on their plans, they often surprise people with great results. It is because they often strive for perfection not only for themselves but also for their surroundings.

Melancholic is the most emotional out of all temperaments. A person with this temperament is more sensitive and pays attention to everything and everyone around him. They also tend to be unhappy when they feel like they did not do their best. Because of their perfectionist tendencies, anything less than 100 percent is seen as a failure.

Additionally, melancholics find it hard to receive compliments. Because they like working in solitude, they do not seek approval from other people. They work with their own set of standards, which is often too high for themselves. They may also have troubles maintaining relationships because of their struggle to express themselves.

However, it is important to note that while these people are verbally reserved, their minds are active and loud. They often have the most creative ideas in their heads. They may appear to be quiet, but their minds are racing with so many thoughts which they later work on in solitude. Melancholics are smart and innovative.

People with the melancholy temperament need to be more outgoing. They need to surround themselves with people who will show them different adventures in life. They also need to have more confidence and faith in themselves. Setting up unrealistic standards is always detrimental for the melancholics. They need to be reminded that at the end of the day, we all make mistakes but that does not define us. Being too idealistic does nothing but hurt our self-image.

Phlegmatic

Phlegmatic people tend to be relaxed and easy-going. They are laidback and tend to have fun without being too loud or too active. They possess so much empathy, but they opt to hide their emotions because do not like confronting their feelings. Phlegmatic people know how to negotiate and are good at resolving problems by willingly meeting halfway with the other party.

Phlegmatics are very calm and peaceful. It may seem that they have their own flow. They avoid stress by not getting too involved with people or any situation that they think are not good for them. They like maintaining relationships at a cordial level. Phlegmatics are often considered as the very definition of 'chill'.

Because of these traits, phlegmatics can be perceived as submissive. When they are around the people they trust, they often leave the decision-making to them. They also have the tendency to just rely on other people's opinions. Even though they might have a slightly different opinion, phlegmatic people will just choose to keep quiet to avoid any tension or argument.

Because of his calm nature, a phlegmatic is often forgiving. When wronged, he will just let it go believing that the confrontation and the drama are not worth his time and energy. Sadly, phlegmatics are prone to bullying and being taken advantage of.

People in this category need to learn how to assess situations and how to be more assertive. What needs to be addressed and what needs to be let go? Just because you spared yourself from the drama does not mean you addressed the problem. Phlegmatics have to stand up for themselves and realize that not everyone can get away with their wrongdoings. Confrontations are not always a bad thing.

Temperament types help us discover the hidden nature of our behavior. By becoming aware of the strengths and weaknesses of our temperament we gain control over them. We can always choose to act differently than our gut reaction might dictate. But in order to develop this discipline we need to know very well our triggers and habitual responses driven by our temperament.

6
Find Something that Defines You

Achieving that One Thing

We all need something in our lives that we desperately aspire to achieve. Having something that motivates us to wake up in the morning in an inspired mood and pushing us to take action out of choice rather than obligation is a critical aspect of fulfilled life. In his book, Gary Keller reminds us that it is very important that we are aware of our One Thing. He asks, *'What's the one thing you can do such that by doing it, everything else will be easier or unnecessary?'*[1]

Do you remember the question from Chapter 1? *What are the most important things for me to spend my time on?* Both Keller's and this question endorse you to think about the same thing.

Each individual has his own One Thing. We have different values. While it is human nature to desire a lot of things, you will realize that as you grow older, your list is narrowed down to the few things you hold close to your heart.

As this list grows shorter, you can already single out

that One Thing that holds the highest value among the rest. Figuring out your own One Thing is crucial to feel fulfillment in life. Think of it as a maze. If you have an idea where the exit is, you can devise a good game plan. You can identify which turns to take, which direction to follow, and which hurdles you will potentially face. But most importantly, you'll know there is an exit, something's waiting for you there. Everybody is in the maze. Just some of us see a purpose in it and try to explore the maze based on their hope to get to the One Thing. Others just sit in the maze, purposlessly, letting the maze's current condition define their lives.

After finding your own One Thing, the next step is to work your way to it. No matter how impossible you think your ultimate goal is, it will always boil down to the amount of effort you put into achieving it.

But how exactly can we attain our One Thing?

The 80/20 Principle

What does hard work mean? Is it working overtime every day? Is it pushing yourself beyond your limits? Nowadays, many of us have a misconstructed idea of what hard work is. More often than not, we think that if we keep ourselves overly busy until midnight and to the point of exhaustion, we must be doing something right. This thought couldn't be further from reality. Being successful means being able to strategize and use your energy, resources and time wisely.

In other words, proper understanding, planning, and timely execution is the key. Patience is also necessary.

What Is the 80/20 Principle?

The 80/20 principle, also known as the Pareto Principle, proposes that an individual should allocate 20 percent of his efforts to gain 80 percent of results. Conversely, to achieve the other 20 percent of the results would require 80 percent of effort. This means that you have to choose high-leverage activities which will yield great results without requiring too much from you. This principle is not strictly about numbers, but the idea that you have to choose high-impacting activities to put your effort on.

After getting a grasp of what the 80/20 principle is, Keller suggests that you look at your One Thing-achieving strategy's 20 percent efforts side and try to narrow it down even further. Take the 20 percent of the 20 percent and so on until you have arrived to the most vital few actions on the list. Then put your effort and undivided attention on these few actions to work towards your One Thing.

Developing Discipline and Focus

As the saying goes, you can never serve two masters at the same time. In achieving your goals, it is important that you know the essence of prioritizing. Today the concept of multitasking sounds attractive since there are so many things we want to do. But the important activities can never be done right while multitasking. Consequently, we can only multitask 'properly' with activities that do not require too much attention. For example, singing while cooking, walking while talking, among others.

Some people might say that they are multitasking by breathing and blinking at the same time. While this is true in the strict sense of the word multitasking, we have to realize that these are subconscious functions that come from a different side of the brain than where focus comes from. Because it is a natural body function, it does not cause channel conflicts with activities that require attention like studying, working, or cooking.

When it comes to more deliberate activities, you might unconsciously put more attention and effort on the harder activity while keeping the easier activity at bay. This is still considered 'doing two things at the same time'. However, Gary Keller emphasizes that multitasking is not giving your full attention to two things but rather, dividing it. Thus we don't really grasp either of them.

Turning Discipline into a Life-Long Habit

Bad habits are hard to break. But good and healthy habits are just as difficult to break. When you have already programmed yourself to following a successful routine, your body gets in tune with its flow. This is why it is very important to turn your focus to establish long-term habits, and stick to the process of habit development with discipline until the activity becomes second nature.

For instance, allotting thirty minutes of your morning to exercise might require an act of discipline from you in the beginning. But if you stick to it long enough, you will slowly integrated it to your daily schedule. Exercising in the morning can then be considered as your habit. When you miss a morning of exercise, you will notice that your body is naturally looking for it.

The key to creating a habit is by starting small. It might be hard in the beginning, but as you slowly get the hang of it, you will realize that it becomes more natural. To achieve your goals, you have to consistently do things that will lead you to them. Turn your discipline to good habits, and these habits will eventually turn into success.

Questioning Life

Most of the time, we do not realize how powerful our questions are. The quality of questions we ask ourselves and the people around us determine the quality of answers we have about life.

One example of a powerful question is Keller's focusing question: *What's the One Thing you can do such that by doing it everything else will be easier or unnecessary?* Forming answers to this question can lead a person to make life-changing decisions. Indeed, questioning life and everything around us allows us to open multiple doors of realization.

Breaking down Keller's focusing question, we can look at it on three different tiers.

First is the part where you ask: *'What's the one thing I can do…'*. This segment allows you to explore your capabilities and skills. It implores you to identify a goal and take action to achieve it. *Can* being the operative word implying that you are acting within your strength and not imposing on yourself as the words *should* or *must* might imply.

Next is the part of *'…such by doing it…'*. This second part talks about purpose. You are acknowledging that by doing that one thing, you are going to get results. This is where you also start to mentally list down the steps that you can take to achieve that goal.

The last segment is *'… everything else will be easier or unnecessary?'* This final part talks about leverage. Here, you recognize that this one thing is something that is highly advantageous for you. It also makes you realize that this one thing should be kept a priority, because it can potentially make everything else in your life lighter and easier.

Keller believes that this focusing question should be asked both on a macro and micro level. It means that you take both small and big steps to achieve a certain goal. For example, if your ultimate goal in life is to be a model, your macro-level step is to create a portfolio and sign up for a modelling agency. On a micro-level, you can start by going on a healthy diet and grooming yourself. Think of the micro level as your everyday plan that will eventually lead you to that macro level.

There are many other life questions that are beneficial to identifying which life direction we should take. These questions can be spiritual, professional, or emotional in nature. When choosing the questions to ask ourselves and others, this quote should always be kept in mind: *'How we phrase the questions we ask ourselves determines the answers that eventually become our life.'* Gary Keller

Setting Goals and Embracing Changes

Goal-setting means that you are connecting your future to the present. You are creating a pathway that you can take to get to your ultimate goal. Most of us think that the future is an isolated place that we need to jump to. However, the future is nothing but connected lines that we need to tread.

Gary Keller additionally believes that achieving success follows a domino effect. You line up your dominoes, from the smallest to the biggest goal, and try to knock them down one by one. You can name your domino pieces as your daily, weekly and monthly goals. After knocking them down, you can move on to the broader ones such as the one-year and five-year goals. Keep knocking these dominoes down until you reach your One Thing.

Setting up goals for yourself requires an immense amount of consistency. If you set up a daily goal, you need to will yourself to do it every single day. Know what you need to do and when you need to do it. Strive to be an efficient and effective worker. As Peter Drucker said, 'efficiency is doing the thing right, effectiveness is doing the right thing.'

Changes

The hard truth about goal-setting is that it entails a whole lot of changes. Some situations even call for a complete self-overhaul. Change is scary because changing ourselves begins with changing our mindset. Life-long, ingrained beliefs don't go away overnight. Also, accepting the need for change includes the acknowledgement that we've been wrong before. Keller explains that most people have an entrepreneurial (E) mindset. In order to be more productive and efficient about goal achievement, we should adopt a purposeful (P) mindset.

To illustrate the difference between E and P mindsets, let's take a look at this example:

When two people are asked to clear out several cups on the table, a person with an E mindset will start right away by picking two cups each time and going back and forth to the sink. A person with a P mindset on the other hand will look for a tray or a big plate to put the cups on so he can clear them out all at once.

Accountability

Embarking on a journey of changing oneself can be tedious. There will always be bad days wherein you feel like you're not making any progress. Other times, you might feel like you are constantly failing to achieve your goals. When this happens, it is so easy to make excuses and justify why we failed. However, keep in mind that successful people know how to be accountable for their actions.

We all have the tendency to make excuses for ourselves to escape pain. We can make up cunning ideas about why everything and everyone is at fault for our failure but us. After all, failing is a really bitter pill to swallow. But if you want to be successful in life, allow yourself to be accountable not only for the good times but also the bad times. Be accountable for both the process and the outcome. When you do this, you are showing yourself and the world that you have a responsible ownership of your life.

One example of taking full charge of your life is knowing when to say yes and when to say no. Distractions can be everywhere especially when you are working. Saying no to a Friday night out to work on your business is one great embodiment of your life ownership. By doing so, you stand your ground as the captain of your own life.

When it comes to your success list, studies show that people who write down their goals are more likely to succeed. People who write them down and share them to other people have even higher chances. This is because they are utilizing the power of accountability. Since they have already let some people know about their aspirations, they are much more motivated to achieve them and prove themselves.

Common Causes of Unproductivity

Sometimes, even though we have all the intention to succeed, we fall short because of distractions. As mentioned in the previous sections, intention is nothing if you do not support them with actions. Your future is not decided by your eagerness but rather what you do with that eagerness. Forming healthy habits and avoiding distractions are the key to your success.

1. **Inability to Say No:** Always saying yes to people can lead to submission and resentment. In his book, Keller strongly recommends that we avoid saying yes to activities that are not related to our One Thing when we are scarce in time and resources. If you feel like it is something that will not make any contribution to your goals and ultimately your life, it is better to say no and spend your time doing more productive things. For example, going out to that extra beer night, sitting in front of the TV out of immediate comfort won't make you happier or more fulfilled.

    Saying no to people especially those whom we are close with can be a challenge. While it is uncomfortable sometimes, you can still decline invitations in a respectful and kind way. Seth Godin said that it is better to bear that short-term pain of saying no rather than the long-term effect of saying yes to something you are not interested in.

    Saying no is equally important to saying yes. Life

fulfillment is not about experiencing everything but experiencing the important things. And you get to decide which things are of value for you and which ones are not. As Steve Jobs once said, 'You'd think focus means saying yes, but it actually means to say no'.

Because distractions can be everywhere, how you position yourself in front of others is crucial. If you make yourself appear always available to other people, chances are you will always be at the top of their minds when they need someone to help them or accompany them. Create the image of a person who values his time. This way, you can reduce incoming requests and low-level distractions.

2. **Poor Health Habits:** Keller believes that personal energy mismanagement is a silent thief of productivity. Consider your health as your fuel. If you run low on energy, there is no way that you can be at the top of your game. Your success is directly proportional to the quality of your health.

   Being successful means knowing how to take care of one's self. Include physical activities, healthy diet and meditation to your daily routine. Aside from the physical body, take care of your emotional and mental health. Meeting up with people who have positive effect on you is a good way to boost your mental energy.

3. **Unsupportive Environment:** There is nothing more distressing than knowing you have all the will to succeed

but your environment hinders you from doing so. If you live with people who are very unsupportive of your changes, it is time to look for another environment. If there is one thing I am sure of, it is that you can never find success in the same place where you are always brought down.

The key is to surround yourself with people who inspire you to become better. Be friends with people who are out of your league. Be motivated by their experiences and their different perspectives. Spend time with those who you know will be supportive of who you want to become. Let your success be inspired and ignited by other people's success too.

The Whole Journey

Nobody can ever achieve success overnight. Becoming the best version of yourself is an everyday and life-long process. Taking down each hurdle to achieve your ultimate goal is a long journey. Be patient, consistent, and hardworking. Believe in the power of determination. No dream is too big for a determined heart.

In this light, I want to include an excerpt from Gary Keller's book:

'I want you to do something. I want you to close your eyes and imagine your life as big as it can possibly be. As big as you have ever dared to dream, and then some.

> *Can you see it? Now, open your eyes and listen to me. Whatever you can see, you have the capacity to move toward. And when what you go for is as vast as you can possibly envision, you'll be living the biggest life you can possibly live. Living large is that simple.'*

Keller's message emphasizes the power of faith and believing. Coupled with hard work, any person can achieve his 'someday goal' when he fully commits to it. This is what it means to be on a journey to success. You dream, you believe in your dream, you try, you fail, and then you try again until you reach that goal.

When you seek out your one thing, it is important that you believe in its purpose. Your faith will be your strength when things get rough. Because you believe in your dreams, you pull through with every obstacle. When you have trust in yourself and you know the worth of your dreams, it becomes easier for you to fight for it. This leads to a journey without regrets.

No Regrets

In his book, Keller included an excerpt of Bronnie Ware's 'The Top Five Regrets of the Dying'. He recognizes the importance of presenting different regrets that a person experiences in his lifetime. These top five regrets are:

1. *'I wish that I'd let myself be happier.'*
2. *'I wish I'd stayed in touch with my friends.'*

3. *'I wish I'd had the courage to express my feelings.'*
4. *'I wish I hadn't worked so hard.'*
5. *'I wish I'd had the courage to live a life true to myself, not the life others expected of me.'*

These statements aim to be a wake-up call to people who take their time on earth for granted. Working hard does not mean abandoning family and friends. Gaining success does not mean losing connection with people or ourselves. A truly fulfilled person is like that because she knows how to find the right balance between work and personal life.

Money cannot buy you happiness and does not equal success. You can't monetize success or feelings. What good will your bank account do when your daughter has become distant from you? Will your promotion save your failing marriage? Your work can never equate to your family and friends.

When you climb the ladder of success, you have to bring your people with you. You cannot leave them on the ground for a while and expect them to still be there when you climb back down after reaching the top. People get tired of forgotten anniversary dates, missed recitals, or not having you around when they need you.

As you work on your one thing, make sure that you explore the most efficient and effective approach to achieve them. Know your priorities, know your limits.

Closing Words

Indeed, having full awareness of who you are as a person will give you life-changing benefits. It is because you are in tune with the desires of your inner self and you are able to take action. You become more productive and efficient when you are able to identify a goal that you can set your eyes onto.

In the first three chapters, we tried to address the feeling of inadequacy—a struggle that most of us face on a daily basis. We concluded that in order to get rid of the feeling of inadequacy, we need to first learn to know and accept our true selves. By doing so, we can take ownership of our strengths and control our weaknesses. And because we are finally aware of who we really are, we do not bother comparing ourselves to others.

We also dived into the topic of personality; personality types, how we can get to know ourselves better based on the characteristics that we have. This helps us to understand not only ourselves but also, the people around us. Becoming aware of what motivates certain behaviors, we can extend utmost understanding and empathy to every being including ourselves. This is a vital part of building relationships.

In chapters four, five, and six, we moved on to using the knowledge of self to train ourselves into becoming our own

Closing Words

better versions. We learned about love languages, apology languages, and human temperaments. These are crucial information as we go on a journey of self-change. We can use our understanding of love and apology languages to cultivate more meaningful conversations with a partner. Our knowledge of temperaments can also help us to assess why we or other people react in a certain manner.

Lastly, we talked about achieving success through Gary Keller's One Thing principle. Before we can set any goals for ourselves, it is important that we are aware of our strengths and weaknesses. Our knowledge of self will serve as our parameter of how far we can go in terms of working towards these goals.

What do I want to achieve in my career? In my relationships?

Can I do it?

What are my strong areas? My limitations?

Being in harmony with our inner self makes it easier for us to identify our own 'One Thing' and be able to work for it.

As I have said in the first chapter, this book does not guarantee that your worries will magically go away. Rather, it aims to serve as a companion and advisor as you go through them. From knowing your personality type to creating your own pathway to success, I hope this book has guided you a lot in discovering yourself and utilizing that self for the better.

References

Akpos, Luckinson. Types of Temperament: Know Why You Behave The Way You Do. Flatimes. 2016. https://flatimes.com/four-types-temperament-know-why-you-behave-way-you-do/

AlleyDog. Carl Jung. AlleyDog. 2018. https://www.alleydog.com/glossary/definition.php?term=Carl+Jung

Allport, Floyd H. Allport, Gordon W. Personality Traits: Their Classification And Measurement. (1921) Psych Classics. First Published in Journal of Abnormal and Social Psychology, 16, 6-40. https://psychclassics.yorku.ca/Allport/Traits/

American Psychological Association. Personality. American Psychological Association. 2018. https://www.apa.org/topics/personality/

Aurum. About Temperaments. The Four Temperaments. 2014. http://fourtemperaments.com/277-2/#1458881176645-9e892f9e-02a0

Aurum. Fundamental Concepts. The Four Temperaments. 2014. http://fourtemperaments.com/277-2/#1458024673600-ff5eb4e5-2009

Briley, D. A., Tucker-Drob, E. M. (2014). 'Genetic and environmental continuity in personality development: A meta-analysis'. Psychological Bulletin. 140 (5): 1303–31. doi:10.1037/a0037091. PMC 4152379. PMID 24956122

References

Chapman, Gary. The Five Love Languages. Northfield Publishing. 2014.

Chapman, Gary. Thomas, Jennifer. When Sorry Isn't Enough. Northfield Publishing. 2013.

Cherry, Kendra. Can You Change Your Personality? Verywell Mind. 2018. https://www.verywellmind.com/can-you-change-your-personality-2795428

Cherry, Kendra. What Are the Id, Ego, and Superego? Verywell Mind. 2018. https://www.verywellmind.com/the-id-ego-and-superego-2795951

Cherry, Kendra. What Is Personality and Why Does It Matter? Verywell Mind. 2018. https://www.verywellmind.com/what-is-personality-2795416

Cowan, G., & Mills, R. D. (2004). Personal inadequacy and intimacy predictors of men's hostility toward women. Sex Roles, 51(1), 67-67+. Retrieved from: http://search.proquest.com/docview/225366434?accountid=1229

Cuddy, Amy. Presence. Orion. 2015

Dweck, Carol. Mindset. Robinson. 2017.

Goddard, Mark. Coping With Feelings of Inadequacy. Health Guidance. 2018. https://www.healthguidance.org/entry/17922/1/coping-with-feelings-of-inadequacy.html

Hendel Jacobs, Hilary. What is the Change Triangle? Hilary Jacobs Handel. 2018. https://www.hilaryjacobshendel.com/what-is-the-change-triangle-c18dd

Jung, C. G. (1971). Psychological types (Collected works of C. G. Jung, volume 6, Chapter X)

Keller, Gary. The One Thing. John Murray. 2013.

Lutz, Peter L. (2002). The Rise of Experimental Biology: An Illustrated History. Humana Press. p. 60. ISBN 0-89603-835-1.

Manson, Mark. The Most Important Question Of Your Life. Mark Manson. 2013. https://markmanson.net/question

McLeod, Saul. Defense Mechanisms. Simply Psychology. 2017. https://www.simplypsychology.org/defense-mechanisms.html

McLeod, Saul. What are the most interesting ideas of Sigmund Freud? Simply Psychology. 2018. https://www.simplypsychology.org/Sigmund-Freud.html

Merenda, P. F. (1987). 'Toward a Four-Factor Theory of Temperament and/or Personality'. Journal of Personality Assessment. 51: 367–374.

Monticello. Thomas Jefferson's Attitudes Toward Slavery. Monticello. 2018. https://www.monticello.org/site/plantation-and-slavery/thomas-jeffersons-attitudes-toward-slavery

Myers, Isabel Briggs; McCaulley Mary H.; Quenk, Naomi L.; Hammer, Allen L. (1998). MBTI Manual (A guide to the development and use of the Myers Briggs type indicator) (3rd ed.). Consulting Psychologists Press. ISBN 0-89106-130-4.

Pittenger, David J (2005). 'Cautionary comments regarding the Myers-Briggs Type Indicator'. Consulting Psychology Journal: Practice and Research. 57 (3): 210–21. doi:10.1037/1065-9293.57.3.210.

Sincero, Sarah Mae. Personality. Explorable. 2018. https://explorable.com/personality

The Myers&Briggs Foundation. MBTI Basics. The Myers&Briggs Foundation. 2018. https://www.myersbriggs.org/my-mbti-personality-type/mbti-basics/home.htm?bhcp=1

Endnotes

Chapter 1: What Brought You to This Book?

1. Cowan, G., & Mills, R. D. (2004). Personal inadequacy and intimacy predictors of men's hostility toward women. Sex Roles, 51(1), 67-67+. Retrieved from: http://search.proquest.com/docview/225366434?accountid=1229
2. Cuddy, Amy. Presence. Orion. 2015
3. Hendel Jacobs, Hilary. What is the Change Triangle? Hilary Jacobs Handel. 2018. https://www.hilaryjacobshendel.com/what-is-the-change-triangle-c18dd
4. Goddard, Mark. Coping With Feelings of Inadequacy. Health Guidance. 2018. https://www.healthguidance.org/entry/17922/1/coping-with-feelings-of-inadequacy.html
5. Monticello. Thomas Jefferson's Attitudes Toward Slavery. Monticello. 2018. https://www.monticello.org/site/plantation-and-slavery/thomas-jeffersons-attitudes-toward-slavery
6. Manson, Mark. The Most Important Question Of Your Life. Mark Manson. 2013. https://markmanson.net/question

Chapter 2: On Personality

1 American Psychological Association. Personality. American Psychological Association. 2018. https://www.apa.org/topics/personality/
2 Cherry, Kendra. What Is Personality and Why Does It Matter? Verywell Mind. 2018. https://www.verywellmind.com/what-is-personality-2795416
3 Briley, D. A., Tucker-Drob, E. M. (2014). 'Genetic and environmental continuity in personality development: A meta-analysis'. Psychological Bulletin. 140 (5): 1303–31. doi:10.1037/a0037091. PMC 4152379. PMID 24956122
4 Sincero, Sarah Mae. Personality. Explorable. 2018. https://explorable.com/personality
5 Cherry, Kendra. Can You Change Your Personality? Verywell Mind. 2018. https://www.verywellmind.com/can-you-change-your-personality-2795428
6 Dweck, Carol. Mindset. Robinson. 2017.

Chapter 3: Freud vs. Jung

1 McLeod, Saul. What are the most interesting ideas of Sigmund Freud? Simply Psychology. 2018. https://www.simplypsychology.org/Sigmund-Freud.html
2 Cherry, Kendra. What Are the Id, Ego, and Superego? Verywell Mind. 2018. https://www.verywellmind.com/the-id-ego-and-superego-2795951
3 McLeod, Saul. Defense Mechanisms. Simply Psychology. 2017. https://www.simplypsychology.org/defense-mechanisms.html